BEACH GAMES
AT THE SHORE

Fun Family Games
for your Shore Vacation

John Focht

Dedication

To Emily and Jack,
who taught me it was okay to dream again.

Acknowledgement

To my family and friends who put up with me over the years as I cheated my way through wiffle ball games, horseshoe games, and rounds of miniature golf at the Shore.

The times at the Shore are memories I will keep with me forever, whether they are the days on the beach in Ocean City, or the nights in Avalon, or anything in between. Thanks to everyone who contributed in one way or another to these games through the years – I think you know who each of you are.

And special thanks to the team at Jera Publishing in Roswell, GA for their expert and professional advice and guidance for this first time author.

About the Author

John Focht is a freelance writer from the Philadelphia area. *Beach Games at the Shore* is his first published book. You can stay up to date on John as he is currently in the process of writing his second book, which is due out in publication in 2014.

Read John regularly on his website at www.JohnFochtJr. com or follow him on Twitter at @JohnFochtJr.

Contents

INTRODUCTION

Ah, our summer vacations at the Shore. You spend most of the year dreaming about kicking back on your beach chair with a cold drink in the sand next to you, while listening to the gentle sounds of the ocean waves crashing in the distance. Your Shore vacation is the time you intend to catch up on that trashy novel you've been longing to read for the past year, or just chillin' at the beach and not doing a thing. The day-to-day grind of the office, the bills, and the household chores are far behind you. The only thing on your mind is the cold Corona sitting next to you in the sand as the sun sets in the distance on another gorgeous day at the beach.

Then reality comes crashing down on you like a tidal wave: "Mom, I don't know what to do!" "Dad, I'm bored, there's nothing to do here." Or "Do we have to go the beach again today?!?"

Ah, the *family vacation* at the Shore. Not quite like the shore vacations of yester-year when the only thing you needed to worry about was turning over on your beach towel so your tan didn't look two-toned, or making sure you had enough ice in your cooler to keep your beverages cold enough to get through the afternoon sun.

Shore days are a bit different now. Just because they are different though, doesn't mean they aren't just as fun – okay, maybe they should be called a different kind of fun.

Beach Games at the Shore can be described as a Shore vacation survival guidebook for your days on the beach. The suggestions in here are beach games and beach activities you probably played yourself as a child.

It's a collection of beach games and beach ideas for the family. Whether it's for the older kids, the little ones, or even for a couple of you uncles out there who just need to get off your beach chair once and while. There are also a few beach add-ons to throw into the mix while you are enjoying your week or two at the Shore. Be sure to pack this book along with you on your Shore vacation this year. Drop it in the beach bag and be ready for your week ahead!

So, kick back and relax, its vacation time!

BALL GAMES AND TOSS GAMES

Days at the Shore can be filled with some of the most memorable family moments while on vacation: swimming in the ocean, the walks along the beach, sitting back and enjoying the day. But what can really provide a lifetime of family memories is an afternoon of beach wiffle ball, or beach skee ball, or beach paddle ball tournaments!

Ball games on the beach are some of the best ways to spend your days while enjoying an afternoon in the sun and enjoying your vacation at the Shore. These beach games are great fun when the entire family is involved. So, it's time to get your crazy aunt off her beach chair and drag her into the game. At the very least, she can take the pictures.

BEACH WIFFLE BALL:

I don't know of a better beach sport to start this section with than *Beach Wiffle Ball*. Whether it is a full game with five to six players or more per side, or a game of one vs. one or two vs. two, always have the wiffle ball and bat ready to go when you go to the beach.

Wiffle ball games that field at least five players on each team should be played with typical baseball rules:

three strikes, three outs. Although, to keep the game moving and keep it competitive, a two-strike, two-out per inning game may suffice.

Teams typically argue whether walks should be allowed in wiffle ball – walks should be allowed if you are using the ol' beach chair as the catcher.

Place a beach chair in the catcher's position behind home plate. When the pitcher pitches, if the pitched-ball hits any part of the beach chair, it is a strike. The pitch has to make it to the beach chair in the air in order to be a strike.

If the pitch misses the beach chair, and the batter does not swing, it is a ball. Of course, any swing-and-a-miss by the batter is a strike. The beach chair keeps the game moving and forces the pitcher to pitch for strikes. It also allows for those knee-buckling wiffle ball curve balls and wiffle ball drop-pitches to be strikes. When choosing teams, make sure you have that Old, Crafty Uncle on your team. Old Uncles always seem to make the best wiffle ball pitchers.

Typical beach wiffle ball games last about three innings, or at least that's about the amount of time before the afternoon sun has zapped most of the players' energy away. Regardless of whether you're playing two vs. two or five vs. five, two or three outs per inning, be sure to set the ground rules prior to the first pitch.

With any wiffle ball game, "beaming" is allowed and should always be allowed – we're talking about a wiffle ball here! Beaming is throwing the ball at the runner in addition to tagging them out or throwing to the fielder covering the base. For safety of course, any beaming in the head is an automatic safe.

In addition to beaming, Pitchers Poison should be used in the one vs. one and two vs. two games. Pitchers Poison allows the defensive players to either throw the ball to the pitcher, or get to the pitchers box prior to the runner reaching base. With limited players in the field, it is a must in these games.

Wiffle ball is also one of the great one vs. one, two vs. two, or even three vs. three beach games too. The rules can vary slightly for these games. The beach chair catcher is essential. For a real tough game, make it either a one-strike, one-out per inning game, or two-strikes, two-out per inning game. This forces the batters to swing and ends the game strategy of trying to walk your way to victory. If you are playing these rules, a minimum of seven innings is usually needed, but you should plan on a nine inning game. These games usually favor the defensive teams.

The one vs. one and two vs. two games can also be played at a much more relaxed pace. After all, this is a book is intended for "North of 40 Crowd" too. For the couch potato wiffle ball players out there (and you know who you are), you can enjoy a three inning game without even breaking a sweat.

Make markers in the playing field for a single, double, triple, and home run (as well as foul lines too). The beach chair catcher is 100% required in this game. After the ball is hit, if it travels in the air to the single mark, it's a single. If it travels in the air to the double marker, it's a double – same for triple and home run.

Balls hit on the ground can also be outs as long as the defensive player catches the ball prior to the ball stopping and does not allow the ball to pass them. There is no running required in this game; just the occasional jog from playing the field while on defense to sitting on your comfortable beach chair with your favorite drink next to you while your team is at bat.

Now, Play Ball!

RUN the BASES:

For the baseball enthusiasts in the family, **Run the Bases** is an absolute Shore event. Although, you don't have to be a baseball enthusiast to play, you don't even need to be a sports enthusiast, heck, you don't even need to have an athletic ability in your body. Run the Bases is a fun beach game to get the whole family and group involved in.

The only thing required for Run the Bases is a ball; it can be a tennis ball, a paddle ball, or a rubber ball. Draw two boxes in the sand at least 20–25 feet from each other. Two people (usually the Dad's) start the game by manning each base and throwing the ball back and forth to each other.

The runners – usually the kids – try to steal the bases safely, while the throwers try to get them out. The game can be played with the runners getting three outs or one out. Once a runner gets their third out (or first, depending on the rules established), they are now the thrower. Whichever thrower tagged the runner for their final out typically switches places with the person who was tagged out.

For the older Dad's, like me, it's usually more enjoyable to remain a steady-thrower, instead of the runner. For the younger Dad's, you will probably enjoy getting in there and swiping a bag or two – but just wait until you hit 40! You'll soon realize being the steady-thrower is the way to go.

One of the enjoyable parts of Run the Bases is you will always pick up a kid or two (or three or four) to join the game. Run the Bases turns into a great way for kids to meet each other on the beach too. You may have also just set your child up with a beach friend for the week.

After about 20 minutes, complete exhaustion usually ends the game with the sweaty, sandy competitors jumping into the ocean!

GAME of CATCH:

Sometimes life is just this simple – a classic game of **Catch**. It can be with two or more people, and all you need is a ball. Stretch the game of catch across the beach and have a game of long toss.

Taking the catch into the ocean makes it that much more enjoyable. Diving into the waves trying to catch the ball is fun and entertaining no matter what your age. It's always great to make that amazing catch into the wave, hold up your arm from under the water and show you made the impossible catch!

HOT CORNER:

Hot Corner takes the game of catch and puts a little competition into it. Hot Corner can be played with two people or more. The rules are simple: throw the ball to the other person, or the next person, if playing with multiple people. If the person catches the ball in the air, they get two points. If they catch it on a bounce, they get one point. If the person catches it on more than one bounce, or they don't catch it, they get zero points. First to 100 points wins.

If playing with multiple people, decide beforehand the rotation of who is throwing to whom. Hot Corner can be played with a tennis ball or rubber ball. It can also be played with a soccer ball or volley ball. For the real enthusiast, trying playing with a football and see how hard it will be to catch on one bounce with the bounce rotation of the football.

For a real challenge though, try Hot Corner with no set rotation. Stay on your toes because you'll never know when the ball will be coming to you next!

Take the game into the ocean. All catches must be in the air when playing in the ocean. Flip the rules around and give two points for a catch and five points if you catch the ball while diving into a wave.

BEACH SKEE BALL:

A great boardwalk and arcade game is skee ball. But skee ball is also a great beach game too. Skee ball is similar to bowling except the player aims to get the ball to fall into a hole rather than knock down pins.

To start, etch out the playing surface with a shovel in the sand. Once you have the playing surface outlined, get a couple of the kids to help smooth out the playing surface; unlike the real game of skee ball, there is no ramp in **Beach Skee Ball**. The kids enjoy building the skee ball surface as much as actually playing it.

Dig a couple of holes into the playing surface. Don't forget to assign a point system to each hole, with the easier holes to hit being worth less points than the more difficult holes.

Build a wall behind the back portion of the playing surface – this will keep the ball from rolling down the beach after each turn, and keep the game from quickly fizzling out once the players realize they have to keep chasing the ball after each turn.

Build the gutter in and around the playing surface too, just like the gutter in the actual game. From there, it's game on. You can play two teams; one vs. one; or just one player. For the most fun results, play with at least three to five balls. Teams or players should alternate rolling the balls down the beach lane toward the holes. First team to 21 wins.

Just like Run the Bases, beach skee ball is a great game for your kids to be entertained, but usually gets the interest of the other kids on the beach who join in. Beach Skee Ball is a great way to get everyone involved and a fun way to spend the day.

BEACH PADDLE BALL:

Of course anyone who has been to the Shore has seen a *Beach Paddle Ball* game. It's the game with two paddles and a pint-sized ball that is sold at every five-and-ten and boardwalk shop in every beach town.

Traditionally, beach paddle ball is a game played between two players, or a team of two vs. two as they volley the ball back and forth. Successfully volleying that tiny ball back and forth is not as easy it sounds though. The ball cannot bounce and sometimes it is tough to get any momentum going.

To make paddle ball an enjoyable beach game, use a racquetball instead of the tiny paddle ball. I know, I know, the paddle ball enthusiasts out there consider this cheating, but a racquetball has got a great bounce.

Draw a court in the hard sand and you can play a great game of beach paddle ball (or may even call it beach tennis). Much like tennis or even Ping-Pong, you must successfully hit the ball in the air over your half of the court. The ball can only bounce one time on your opposition's side of the court. If the ball bounces more than once, or if it bounces off the court, the point is yours. If the ball travels in the air and does not bounce on your opponent's court, and your opponent does not swing at it, the point belongs to them. The game is played to 21, and you must win by two.

Using a racquetball makes a volley-back-and-forth game a bit more manageable since the ball can bounce. It can also really draw up interest with everyone in the family. Create a family tournament and see who gets bragging rights for the next year as Beach Paddle Ball Champion.

Okay, okay, so this is not the true way beach paddle ball is intended to be played, but it is fun. Of course the actual game of paddle ball (played with the tiny paddle ball itself) is just as enjoyable. The rules are relatively the same as mentioned above with using the racquetball, but the significant difference is the ball cannot bounce. True beach paddle ball can be played in either the hard or soft sand.

Another great way to enjoy paddle ball is a simple game of volley back and forth between two players. After all, not all beach games must be a competitive battle. Volley the paddle ball back and forth between two players and see how many consecutive volleys you can get. Keep score and see if you can break your record of consecutive volleys.

If you do have more than two players, get challenges going and break the groups into teams. See which team can get the most volleys in the air. Although it is a competitive game, you'll enjoy going against teams to see which team can keep the volley going longer.

Beach paddle ball can also be played with just one player. See how many times you can consecutively hit the ball in the air. Then, try to break the previous mark. You'll be surprised to see how many in the family or group want to join in to see who can set the single-person volley record for this day.

HORSESHOES:

Okay, so we've found a few ways to entertain the kids on the beach for hours each day, but what about the rest of us, you know, the parents?

If you have your binoculars you can sightsee all day – I'm talking about looking out into the ocean at the sailboats and dolphins, of course. But there has to be something else to do that doesn't require all the physical movement and activity as wiffle ball and paddle ball. We are supposed to be on vacation, right?

Horseshoes may have been invented by the ancient Greeks, but it was made to be played at the Shore between dads, moms, uncles, aunts, grandparents, and even the kids.

Horseshoes is an outdoor game played between two people, or two teams of two people, using four horseshoes and two sets of stakes set into the ground – or in this case into the beach.

Horseshoes is actually a very competitive game with official rules and scoring, but since we are talking beach horseshoes here, the rules of can be tweaked a bit to make the game a more enjoyable beach-time activity. However, for those of you who are ultra-competitive about your horseshoes, review the *Rules of the Game as governed by the National Horseshoes Pitchers Association* on the NPHA website for official rules and scoring.

When horseshoes is played between two people, the players stand on the same side and individually toss their horseshoe at the opposite stake which has been staked into the beach surface. Who throws first can be determined by each player throwing an initial toss of horseshoes to see who gets closer to the stake, or it can simply be decided by a game of rock-paper-scissors – this is your choice.

If you are playing teams, a player from each team should be opposite each other; for example, one side contains a player from Team A and Team B, and the other side also contains a player from Team A and Team B.

Official rules of horseshoes state a horseshoe must lie within six feet of the stake. If each team throws a toss and the horseshoes land exactly the same distance within the six feet, the throws cancel each other out and no one gets the point. Whoever gets closer to the stake, and is within the six feet, gets the point. A ringer is worth three points. Play to 21.

Sometimes playing with the kids though, it's tough to get the 'shoe within six feet of the stake. To avoid a three-hour game of horseshoes, make it closest to the stake, even if the closest horseshoe lands 10–15 feet from the stake. Play the game to 21 and pitch away the afternoon.

WASHERS:

A game similar to horseshoes is the game **Washers,** which can also be played one vs. one, or two vs. two. Washers is played by tossing washers at a box that contains a can and its scoring is very similar to that of horseshoes in that the players attempt to toss their washers near the box, onto the box, or in the can.

Players receive one point if a washer lands within a foot of the box or is leaning against the box. Three points if the washer lands on the box. Five points if the washer lands inside the can. Only one player can score per round.

The team or player that scores in the previous round throws first in the next round.

SHELL HORSESHOES:

Of course, it doesn't always work out that you are actually carrying a set of horseshoes or a game of washers with you to the beach each day. This is where years of wisdom and your parent ingenuity kicks in – let's play a game of **Shell Horseshoes**! The rules for shell horseshoes combine those of horseshoes and washers, but with some minor differences in the playing gear.

First, find yourself four hardy shells along the beach, shells that are strong enough and can withstand being tossed around the beach for the next 30 minutes or so.

Once you've found your four playing shells, dig two holes in the ground, roughly the same distance you would have dug the stakes in the ground if you had a set of horseshoes. Viola! Instant shell horseshoes.

Not only do you have a game for yourself and the other adults, but it's a game the kids love more so than the actual horseshoes game because it seems more clever to them – you're an instant hit with the kids too!

CORNHOLE:

Cornhole is a great summertime game that can be played at backyard barbeques and picnics. Cornhole is much like washers and horseshoes. The objective of cornhole is to toss beanbags across a 30-foot playing surface and land them into a hole on a wooden board.

The biggest challenge with cornhole at the beach, however, is lugging around a pair of 2x4 boards with you. After all, between all the beach blankets, chairs, umbrellas, boogie boards, and bags that we carry to the beach each day, who really has the extra hands to carry a couple of extra games?

So, get your family's creative juices flowing and create your own impromptu cornhole game. Like shell horseshoes, you can create your own beach version of cornhole with either objects you find on the beach, like seashells, or with objects that you have brought to the beach with you, like flip-flops!

Instead of using a two-by-four board, draw a two-foot-by-four-foot box in the sand and dig a hole out of the top of the box. March thirty feet across the beach and do the same thing and voila! Instant cornhole playing field!

Just as with the games of horseshoes and washers, cornhole can be played with any members of the families. There is no athletic ability required; maybe just bring your sense of humor to laugh at some of the errant flip-flop tosses that miss the hole by a mile! The game can be played one vs. one, or in teams of two vs. two.

If playing one vs. one, each player takes turns tossing the objects (in this case, the flip-flops) at the other hole. Each player has two flip-flops to toss at the other hole. Whichever player either tosses a flip-flop into the hole, or lands the flip-fop in the box and is closer to the hole, wins the inning or frame. First team to 21 wins.

As with the shell horseshoes, the game is an instant hit with the little kids too! The kids will typically find a ton of enjoyment not only in playing the game, but in more cases than not, coming up with the idea and building the playing surface!

LADDER BALL:

A backyard game and summer picnic game that has swept across the country over the last decade or so is the game of **Ladder Ball**. Ladder ball is a game that seems to have been invented with the intention of getting dads, moms, aunts and uncles off their lounge chairs and into some competitive game action in the summer without causing too much physical exertion. Ladder ball is a terrific game to take along with you to the shore.

The ladders are typically 15–20 feet from each other, but depending on the competition, they can be placed further or closer. It can be played one against one or a team consisting of two players each side. Play to 21 and win by two points.

The scoring system is determined by players landing the tossed bola on a rung of the ladder. Scoring systems vary family to family on how many points each ladder rung is worth. Typically the middle rung is the toughest rung to hit, so that should be worth three points. The bottom rung is the second toughest rung to hit, so that should be worth two points. And the top rung is the simplest rung to hit, so that should be worth one point.

The ruling system sometimes varies from family to family, or instructions included within each game. Whatever ruling system you use, it's another great day at the Shore.

BEACH BOCCE BALL:

One of the ultimate "Old Man" Shore games is **Beach Bocce Ball**. It's a game that requires zero athletic ability, yet keeps dads, uncles, and granddads occupied for hours on the beach. (Moms may want to get this for dads just to keep the dads from bugging *them* all day). Bocce ball is a game that can be played between two players, or two teams. The teams can consist of two, three or four players on each team.

The game, or more precisely the match, is started by one of the teams tossing a smaller ball, called the jack. The team that threw the jack tosses their bocce ball first. Once the first team has tossed their first bocce ball, the other team can toss their first bocce ball. From that point on, it's bocce ball game on!

Whichever bocce ball landed furthest from the jack, that team will throw the rest of their remaining bocce balls. Once all bocce balls have been tossed by Team One, Team Two will now toss their bocce balls at the jack.

The object of bocce ball is to get your teams bocce balls closest to the jack. By tossing second, your team kind of has home field advantage – or should we say home beach advantage.

By tossing second, your team now has the advantage of seeing where Team One tossed their bocce balls and you can plan your attack strategy from there.

The team with the closest bocce ball to the jack, without touching the jack, is the only team that can score points in any frame. The scoring team receives one point for each of their bocce balls that is closer to the jack than the closest ball of the other team. Whichever team wins the frame, tosses the jack in the next frame. First team to thirteen wins.

Of course, strategy is involved when playing beach bocce ball. Consider where on the beach you are playing: hard sand vs. soft sand. When playing on hard sand, the ball will roll, so you'll have to adjust accordingly. A good back spin will be needed, or be sure to toss your ball short of the jack to take into account the role factor.

When playing in the soft sand, the likelihood of a roll is pretty remote. You will need to aim your toss to be as precise to the jack as possible. You may want to consider your opponents' weakness when deciding on playing on the hard sand or soft sand.

For a relatively simple game, there is quite a bit of planning and strategy involved. Bocce ball is a fun beach game to be played with a cooler of beverages nearby, although that can also be a disadvantage as you try to plan out your strategy.

BEACH FOOTBALL:

Okay, enough with the Dad-games and non-athletic beach games already. Let's get some action going! Just like a game of wiffle ball on the beach, **Beach Football** brings the same fun to a beach day with a bit more action-packed intensity to it than horseshoes and bocce ball. Beach football can be played two vs. two or with a full team on both sides. If you have an odd number of players, designate someone steady-quarterback.

Since this isn't the NFL or College Football, the game should be played with simple rules. First downs should be used in beach football, but instead of using ten yards for a first down, use completions in a series. Three completions within a series make up a first down.

Designate rules beforehand to handle blitzes and pass rushes. A good rule of thumb is the old "Five Mississippi Rush" rule. The "Five Mississippi Rush" rule stems from playground football at the school yard. It simply means the defensive player cannot cross the line of scrimmage to rush the quarterback until after he or she has counted to five. The defensive player must count aloud for the quarterback to hear: "One Mississippi, two Mississippi, three Mississippi..." The defensive player must continue counting until they reach Five Mississippi, then they can proceed to rush the quarterback.

The defensive team can only "blitz" once per series. This means they can rush the quarterback without counting to Five Mississippi, but must yell out "BLITZ" as they charge the quarterback.

Split the sides evenly and add some competitive makeup to it – losing team gets dinner that night. Be sure to split the teams evenly to have a competitive makeup on both sides of the ball. Although you will be surprised to find that some of the most competitive players on the field will be the moms and aunts who seem so sweet, but will lay you out in a minute if it means that they don't need to worry about dinner that night.

The end of a beach football game is usually the best. Whether you are playing rough touch, two-hand touch, or tackle, by game's end, everyone is covered in sweat and sand and requires a dip in the ocean. All good beach football games end with a crowd of sandy bodies running down the beach and hurling themselves in the ocean waves.

BEACH VOLLEYBALL:

Typical *Beach Volleyball* games are games played between teams consisting of two players on each side. For the ultra-intense beach volleyballers, or the volleyballers playing in Santa Monica, California, there probably isn't any other way to go. But when at the Shore, a friendly beach game between families or just a group of beach vacationers who want to get off the beach chairs for the afternoon, beach volleyball is a way to play hard and get dirty.

Beach volleyball, when played with more than two players, is played the same as indoor volleyball. It's a less intense game since there are more players on each side who are just enjoying the day, but be aware that there is always that uncle lurking who thinks he is in the Beach Volleyball Olympics and is just waiting to spike the ball at the ten-year-old on the other side of the net.

For the friendly beach games at the Shore, the scoring system should be the team gets a point no matter who serves, otherwise it might make for a long afternoon if only the serving team gets the point.

Although the point system should be "Shore-friendly," be sure you keep the basic rules of the game in play. Teams should rotate when starting a new serve. Teams can only set the ball three times before hitting over the net to the other team, and no consecutive sets by a player.

With the two vs. two matchup, that's where you typically get the ultra-competitive games going. You may see an old sibling-rivalry reborn with a brother-vs.-brother matchup. Best advice here: stay clear and place your bets!

FRISBEE GAMES

A Frisbee seems as much a part of the Shore as the board-walk, the sand, and ocean itself. As you walk up and down the beach, you can find countless Frisbees being tossed through the air – both on the beach and in the ocean. The Frisbee may have been invented in California, but it was created for the Shore.

After all, what is summer and the beach without a game of Frisbee? But we're not talking your grandfa-ther's Frisbee here. While a simple game of Frisbee catch is a ton of fun – particularly if you are having a Frisbee catch with someone who can actually throw a Frisbee! – there are quite a few other Frisbee games to turn a day at the beach into a fun-filled day of beach games.

FRISBEE RUN the BASES:
Let's start with *Frisbee Run the Bases*. The same rules of regular Run the Bases apply to Frisbee Run the Bases except only one out per player until they become the thrower.

There are two principles of the game to keep in mind while you are playing: if you are the runner, there is a good chance to steal as many bases as you wish, particularly if one of the throwers has trouble throwing a Frisbee (you'd be surprised how many people *can't* throw a Frisbee). Also, when you are the runner, keep your head up while you are running. Sometimes those throws from a Frisbee come in low and hard and it's a good way to get whacked if you are not watching where you are running!

FRISBEE GOLF:

Frisbee Golf, or "Frolf" as once referred to by George Costanza, combines Frisbee and golf. Frisbee golf really took off in the 1960s. Today, there is a governing body of Frisbee golf called the *Professional Disc Golf Association* (PDGA). Frisbee golf played on the beach doesn't quite require the same regimented rules as required by the PDGA, but of course some balance of rules and fun are required.

One rule which is pretty standard with Frisbee golf is a wide playing surface. Just as with beach football or a beach wiffle ball, a large and wide enough playing surface is needed. Sometimes Frisbee golf is best played at the end of the day when the beach is less crowded, or early in the morning. This allows for some of those errant throws to sail harmlessly out-of-bounds without the fear of taking off the head of a nearby sunbather.

When playing Frisbee golf as an enjoyable, relaxing day at the beach, you can simply dig holes in the sand to designate the hole. If you have a basket or a bucket, you can also use that, but digging a hole in the sand usually works best for beach Frisbee golf.

When deciding who tees off first on the first hole, make it interesting and race to the ocean, dive in, and see who gets back to hole #1 first and let that determine your playing order.

Just like traditional golf, Frisbee golf is particularly nice to play with a couple of good friends, a cooler of beverages nearby, and some food on the beach blanket for in between holes

FRISBEE FOOTBALL:

Well, since we are on the Frisbee kick, let's keep it going with *Frisbee Football*. Frisbee football is sometimes better played with smaller teams; maybe three vs. three, or four vs. four, but if you have more players, then play the game!

No difference in rules between regular beach football and Frisbee football – well, except the fact you are playing with a Frisbee and not a football. The ultimate part of Frisbee football is you never really no where the Frisbee may go when that quarterback is under pressure from the defense and has to let that Frisbee go. Once it leaves his or her hand, it's anyone's guess where the flying disc will travel from there.

Frisbee football adds some fun to those who want to enjoy a get-out-and-get-at-it type game, but not necessarily in the mood for an actual football game. One additional item with Frisbee football: like some of the other games mentioned here, Frisbee football is best played early in the morning or late in the day when there are not as many people on the beach. You need some space to play, and you need to be cautious of where those errant flips of the disc travel.

FRISBEE BASEBALL:

Can it be? *Frisbee Baseball*? You bet! Frisbee baseball is another of the great beach games to play that doesn't require any athletic ability. Just bring your running game, and practice those Frisbee tosses.

Unlike traditional baseball, you do not need gloves, bats, or any other type of equipment, other than a Frisbee of course. Just draw some boxes in the sand for bases, and some foul lines, and you are set to go.

Just like in wiffle ball, the teams can consist of two against two, or upwards of five, six, seven aside. One team bats, the other team takes the field. Decide beforehand if you are playing one, two, or three outs per side.

The most important rule in Frisbee baseball is that the batter must throw the Frisbee a certain distance for it to be considered a fair ball.

Make it a distance that is fair for everyone playing. A travel distance of thirty feet is a pretty reasonable distance. Draw a fair line in the infield to set the distance. Also draw some foul lines down the first and third baselines to ensure there is distinction between a foul and fair down the lines.

Since there are no pitchers, the only chance of strikeouts is if the batter fouls out. If you are playing with really experienced-level Frisbee throwers, you may want to make one foul a strikeout – this will keep the competition-juices flowing. For the less-experienced, and family-oriented type game (you know, the one that keeps all the kids from fighting), make three fouls a strikeout.

For the defensive players in the field, as with baseball and wiffle ball, anything caught in the air is an out (whether in fair territory or foul).

If the fielder picks the Frisbee off the ground, the fielder can throw to another defensive player who is covering the base the runner is running toward, but the fielder may only take one step and throw to the base.

Unlike baseball, the fielder may not chase down and tag the runner. Also, there is no "beaming" as there is in wiffle ball. This puts the pressure on the fielder to catch the Frisbee in the air – and maybe show off some of those fancy Frisbee catches while you are at it.

And of course, the most important part...FUN. Frisbee baseball is a terrific family beach game, or group beach game. Sure, you need to know how to toss a Frisbee, and catch it, but in the end, Frisbee baseball can surely be enjoyed by your entire beach brigade.

Bring your camera and laughs for this one, because beach Frisbee baseball will bring a ton of memories to be shared all season long.

FRISBEE CATCH:

This book would be remiss if it failed to provide a section to just the simple love of a Frisbee toss. Hours can be dwindled away on the beach with a simple *Frisbee Catch*. From making great tosses to remarkable catches, a simple catch of Frisbee turns a beautiful sunny day on the beach to an afternoon to remember.

The ultimate Frisbee toss is even better in the ocean. Show off those moves with catches into the waves and leaps into the air through the ocean before the flying disc reaches the water. Create lasting shore memories with the kids by teaching them how to toss and catch a Frisbee.

Sands and Hands,
Shovels and Pales

So what about the little ones? We've done the easy part so far with this book. We've talked about all the beach games to play when the kids are a bit older and you can either send them in a direction with a beach game to play, or we've been able to conjure up a game where we can get the whole family involved – even able to get that crazy aunt that every family has into a game.

Sometimes the Shore vacation can be a make-or-break event just by the little ones' reactions to the beach. Let's face it, if the beach is a chore with trying to keep the little ones occupied, or fighting them just to play with the shovel and bucket you brought down for them, it could spell disaster for the next several years for any type of beach days at the Shore.

So, here are some beach activities and tricks to keep in mind when you are dealing with the little ones, and how to get them to enjoy your beach day at the Shore. And maybe more importantly, how to get them to look forward to the Shore for the next several years to come.

DIG a CHANNEL to the OCEAN:

Come on, dads, you know when it comes down to it, you really want to get down in the sand with the kids and dig in the dirt and get all dirty and wet. Well, get off your beach bum and get creative with it. Think bigger than just digging in the sand with the $2 bucket and shovel you just bought at the five-and-dime; the kids can do that on their own – think big!

Digging a Channel to the Ocean might be the easiest thing for dads and moms to do that will require relatively little work, and potentially an afternoon of enjoyment for your little one – and relaxation for you!

All little kids love playing in the sand, but they sometimes get a little bored because after all, how much can even a little one get out of just digging? Our goal as parents is to give them something to dig for.

The stage is pretty simple to set. Just dig out a channel from your beach blanket down to the ocean. Once the channel is dug out, get a bucket of water and pour it from the top of the channel and watch it flow through the channel to the ocean. Then kick back and enjoy as your little ones run up and down the beach from the blanket to the ocean pouring water through the channel back to the ocean's edge.

Have a few buckets on hand and watch as your kids, as well as other kids, join in to keep the water flowing down the channel. Of course, every now and again, your assistance will be required to help dig out the channel, but for the most part, it's an afternoon of enjoyment for you as you watch the kids scamper frantically to keep the water flowing through the Great Channel.

The extra nice part is if you are successful enough in recruiting some of the other little ones from neighboring beach blankets, you've potentially set your little one with a playmate for the week, which of course allows you to kick back and enjoy your beach day a bit more.

FILL a HOLE with WATER:

Can it be that simple? You bet! *Filling a Hole with Water* is simply just flipping up the digging a channel to the ocean a bit. After all, we all know that filling an entire week of digging a channel to the ocean can only go so far. So, an easy way to resolve that problem is just turning it into filling a hole with water.

Let's start with getting off our beach chairs again. Once there, grab a shovel and start digging, and I mean digging. Don't just dig a tiny hole; dig a hole that makes the kids feel they are halfway to the center of the earth. Get the kids to grab their shovels too and help with the hole.

Once the hole meets your specifications, grab the buckets and start the mad dash to fill the hole with water. One of the beautiful parts of this game is it's obviously impossible to keep the hole filled with water – sometimes the kids don't pick up on this right away.

Engage the surrounding kids again and have them bring their gear, i.e., buckets and shovels. Just as with digging the channel to the ocean, children love trying to keep the hole filled. Some of the kids stay in the hole while ocean water is poured over them and into the hole.

As with the channel to the ocean, your services will be needed throughout the afternoon to help dig the hole back out, but for the most part, your investment in this activity is pretty much on auto-pilot.

You've again become the local beach blanket hero. And in the end, you've really just created two of the same game for the kids: channel to the ocean and filling a hole with water. Filling a hole with water, and digging a channel to the ocean also provides your kids alternate games for the week. Both are big hits – for the kids and for you!

BUILD a SLIDE into a DEEP HOLE:

So, since we are on the subject of digging holes, another great beach activity for the little ones is *Building a Slide into that Deep Hole* you just dug out.

As you are digging this monstrous hole, an added bonus is the giant mountain that you are unintentionally creating right next to this gigantic hole. Sometimes, with any great idea, another great idea arises. This giant mound of sand is just that.

Once you have dug out the giant hole, now set your sights on the enormous pile of sand. Start smoothing out a section of the mountain to create a sliding board. Since the mountain is right next to the hole you just dug out, keep having the kids fill the hole with water. Presto! You've got yourself your own personal poolside heaven next to the ocean with a sliding-board into the pool! Who's better than you right now?!?

PADDLE BALL MAZE on a MOUNTAIN of SAND:

It's amazing how much good usage you can get out of a hole on the beach and a giant mountain of sand next to it – only if we could package this up and bring it home with us.

Now it's time to take a paddle ball, or a tennis ball, or any other type of small ball you have brought to the beach with you. Come on, we know you have something in that giant beach bag you carry every day – and I'm talking to the dads here!

Smooth out the giant mountain of sand. Take the paddle ball and begin to carve out a lane from the top of the heap of sand going round and round until it dumps the ball out into the hole. Once the pattern is carved out, place the ball at the top of the mound and let it weave its way round and round to the bottom. If the sand mountain is big enough, carve out multiple lanes for multiple paddle balls to run through.

The kids will enjoy racing the balls down the mountain maze that you have created – again, you've become the beach hero. Now, kick back and enjoy the races.

DRIPPY CASTLES:

Well, if this one sounds pretty basic to you, it's because it is. **Drippy Castles** keep the kids happy. Help them out. Start them out. Sit them down in the sand by the shoreline. Build them a little pile of wet sand, then drip some wet sand on top to form castles and towers. Bingo! Instant entertainment. Instant fun.

Now try drippy castles on their legs. Have your little ones sit on the beach with their legs in front of them. Grab some wet sand and drip it on their legs. You've created drippy castles right on them. Talk about entertainment for a two year old! Not only that, but once they have created their master piece to satisfaction, have them wash it off and do it again! Back and forth in out of the sand and water. What more could you ask for?

Now sit your chair next to them by the ocean and get back to that trashy beach novel you are trying to get through this week!

BUILD a MOAT and a DAM:

Once you're kids have built that beautiful drippy castle, they need to protect it from the ocean. Help dig a trench around the sand castle and build a dam with the sand from the moat. The ocean tide always wins this battle, but the kids enjoy trying to dig and re-dig the moat and build and re-build the dam.

It turns into a beach activity that the kids love. It also turns into a beach sound you'll love as the kids laugh and giggle trying to battle the ocean tide to save to their sand castle. Keep your camera and video-recorder close for this one!

BUILD a CAR in the SAND:

Building a Car or Boat in the Sand is an all-time favorite Dad-thing to do to keep kids occupied for an afternoon on the beach. This doesn't take much at all, except a shovel and a bit of imagination.

Dig two or more rectangular holes in the sand. Make sure that the ends line up and the long edges of the rectangles face each other. Leave enough space in between the rectangles so that the raised sand in between can act as seats and the holes themselves can act as floorboards.

Use the sand that you dug for the holes to build up the front, back, and sides of the car. Use some shells, or shovels, and even some buckets to make up the steering wheel, headlights, mirrors, and doors. And viola, instant car.

Little kids enjoy the car, or boat, more than you could possibly imagine. The nice thing is your car is there all day, so your little ones have something to come back to throughout the course of your beach day.

BURY the KIDS in the SAND:

If you haven't figured this one out yet, it's either your first-ever trip to the Shore, or maybe you should think about a vacation in the mountains next summer. *Burying the Kids in the Sand* is a time-honored tradition that goes back as far as the first beach vacationers. The kids love it; the parents love it; everybody wins!

Dig a deep-enough and wide-enough hole for your child to fit into. Tell them to hop in; keeping their heads out of the hole of course. Start filling the hole back with sand.

One of the enjoyable outcomes here is that after you have buried your child in the sand, they love just sitting in the hole with sand buried up to their heads! Talk about killing an afternoon.

Just as much fun with burying the kids in the sand, is going swimming with them after they dig themselves out. Just as with the beach sports mentioned earlier, there is no way this ends without a dip in the ocean.

When your child finally pulls themselves out of their entombed beach hole, they are beach monsters. Enjoy this opportunity to go swimming with the kids, and not just standing by the shoreline as they swim. Race them down to the ocean and jump in with them. Roll around in the ankle-deep water with your child and at the end of the swim try to figure out who enjoyed it more, you or them.

BUCKET RACES:

Now if you can't get your competitive juices flowing for this one, you might as well just sit back down on the beach chair, tilt the beach umbrella to shield the sun, and just go back to your siesta.

You don't need an athletic bone in your body, or an ounce of sports sense to your being to enjoy **Bucket Races**. It is relay-races with buckets filled with ocean water! Grab the family, and the family sitting next to you for that matter, and get some buckets and let's go!

The object of bucket races is simple: TO WIN! Bucket races is the beach version of the relay-race. Break the family or group into teams; the amount of teams will depend on how many people you have. Break the teams into two sections: one section near the ocean, the other section at the top of the beach.

The team members at the ocean start the race. The object is to carry the filled-bucket of ocean water up to the top of the beach and hand it off to your teammate at the top of the beach. The kicker is, you can't spill any water from the bucket. If you do, you must mark your spot, fill the bucket back up, go back to your spot, and proceed with the bucket race!

The object of the game is whichever team finishes the race first, wins! Make the game ultra-competitive and have the losing team carry all the beach items back to the house at the end of the beach day. The game is easy, and most importantly the game is fun. And remember, sure and steady usually wins the race!

One thing to be aware of when choosing sides: don't pick the uncle who has been sitting next to the cooler of adult beverages all day. The odds of him being able to carry a bucket of water up and down the beach without spilling are pretty remote!

COLLECTING and PAINTING SEASHELLS:

Is there more of a Shore thing to do than collecting seashells? Collecting shells along the beach is a relaxing and enjoyable way to spend a day at the Shore with the family. Be sure to bring a bucket along to carry your beach treasures home with you. (To find the really great shells, head out early in the morning and see what the ocean brought in overnight.)

Once back at the Shore house, go to your five-and-dime and pick up some finger paint or a set of crayons. Let your little ones' creative side flourish by painting and drawing the works of art of the day's collection. You will wind up with something a whole lot more than a bucket of shells; you wind up taking home a bucket of memories.

P.S. – Be sure the kids are painting the shells outside. You don't need to lose your security deposit on spilled finger-paint all over the kitchen table and floor!

FOOTPRINTS:

So you want to keep your child occupied a bit on the beach, as well as try to work off a bit of this morning's five-course breakfast? Start walking in the sand while your child sits on the beach blanket and counts to thirty.

Once at thirty, have your child follow your *Footprints* to try to find you (of course depending on your child's age, they may require some help in counting to thirty and/or following your footprints).

It's a bit like hide-and-seek, or like Marco Polo in the pool, but your child can only find you by following your footprints. The little ones love playing this with Mom or Dad, and it gives Mom or Dad yet another excuse to get off their beach bums and get a little exercise while on their Shore vacation.

Another fun activity along the lines of footprints is picking up a beach watering-can; they are sold with the buckets and shovels at the five-and-dime. Fill the watering-can up with water and make a trail in the sand. Have your little one follow the trail of water to you.

Whether it's the watering-can or footprints, it's always fun when the kids find you hiding in the dunes or behind the lifeguard stand. Just enjoy their reactions!

GRAB a BOOGIE BOARD and CATCH a WAVE:

Go to your local five-and-dime shop, flip $20 on the counter, and buy a boogie board for your child. Letting them loose in the ankle and knee-deep ocean with their boogie board will keep them going all week too.

Now what about you, Mom and Dad? We can't forget about you! To steal a line from The Beach Boys: "Catch a wave and you're sitting on top of the world". No matter your age, you should not let your Shore vacation get away without boogie boarding at least once. When the kids are done, enjoy the feeling of catching that wave and riding it into the shoreline yourself!

SOME MORE MUST BEACH DO'S AT THE SHORE

This book wouldn't be complete if I didn't mention a few additional shore-time activities that need to occur while on your vacation at the Shore. These activities are not necessarily activities that take place on the actual beach, but nonetheless, they need to take place while you are at the Shore.

FLY a KITE:

I'm not sure if there is a better Shore activity for parents and kids than a day at the beach and flying a kite – especially if you catch a nice ocean breeze swirling around the beach.

Flying a kite can keep your child enthralled for hours on the beach. It's also something that you can keep going by tying the kite string to your beach chair and allowing the kite to fly off in the distance all afternoon.

Of course there are days when the breeze isn't as cooperative to your kite flying plans. But with a little patience, you can still get that kite up and watch your children's faces light up when you eventually harness the power of the wind on a beautiful, sunny day at the Shore.

BUILD a STATUE in the SAND of ITEMS YOU HAVE FOUND on the BEACH:

Have you ever walked up and down the beach and just taken notice of all the interesting items that wash up along the shore? We've all seen them, but aside from pretty seashells, who really pays attention to what the ocean waves crash on the shoreline?

Grab a bucket and let's take a walk and find out. Walk the shoreline with your family and collect the seaweed, driftwood, seashells (and not just the pretty shells but the broken ones too), and whatever else the ocean has sent our way that day. Bring them back to your beach blanket and let your creative side take over.

Dump the items out and begin building statues or figures in the sand. Between the shells, the seaweed, the driftwood, and whatever you could carry, you can create quite the beach museum from the items you find on the beach.

If you have collected enough items, after the initial statue is built, have each member of your family keep adding additional items to it. Or once the statue is initially created, break the family into teams to find more beach treasures to add to your statue. Don't forget to take a picture.

MINIATURE GOLF:

No Shore vacation is complete without a round or two of miniature golf. If you have the competitive family, set a day aside for a miniature golf outing. Hit a few of the miniature golf courses and play a tournament to see who wins the most rounds, who shoots for the best score, who gets the most holes-in-one, and who wins the most free games.

Break the family up into teams of four and play three, four, or five different courses in the same day (your choice if the teams have to play the same courses, or just randomly pick their own courses).

At the end of the day, meet back for dinner and tally up the scores. See which team had the best overall score. If the teams are playing the same courses, tally up the team scores from each course to see which team won which course. Tally up the scores at dinner with prizes for the winners. It's a fabulous way to spend the day, and great way to get the family together.

BIKE RIDES:

The one thing about the Shore that seems to happen to all of us – we all seem to suddenly turn into "The Athlete." Must be something about the salt air, but once we are on that Shore, we all suddenly love our walks, our morning jogs, and our bike rides.

Bike riding is a simple way to pull the family together for a morning. Plan a morning to bike to a local break-fast spot. Once you are finished with that large pancake, bacon, and eggs breakfast, jump back on the bikes and pedal around the island.

Decide on a destination before you leave, like biking to the local marina, or biking the boardwalk, or even just biking to the end of the island and back. Good way to get a great meal and burn off those morning calories so you can spend the rest of your day relaxing in your beach chair by the ocean.

KAYAKING:

Keeping the summer athlete motto in mind, let's not forget about kayaking either. Find your local marina, rent a kayak for a few hours, and drift along through the back bays and channels.

Kayaking is fun for the whole family. Rent a few kayaks and spend a summer morning at the Shore visiting parts of the island you typically never see. One useful tip though: when kayaking through the channels of the bay, bring plenty of bug spray. Otherwise the mosquitoes and flies will enjoy your kayaking adventure more so than you!

WATER PARK:

It might sound odd to plan a water park day while on your Shore vacation, but it's a day that won't be forgotten. If your Shore town doesn't have a water park, look at the neighboring towns to find one that does. Plan a half day or a whole day. For those of you not inclined to venture against the four-story water slides, find a tube and float the lazy river for the afternoon.

Everyone always becomes a kid again at the water parks, and you'll be stunned to find yourself hanging with the kids, going up and down the steps to hit the next slide.

The only caution to a fun day today at the water park is, be ready for a painful day tomorrow when your body makes you remember you are not as young as you used to be!

WALK on the BEACH at NIGHT

End your day with an evening walk on the beach. If you are going to dinner, and the restaurant is within walking distance, take off your shoes and walk home on the beach along the waterline.

The beach at night is quiet, peaceful, and beautiful. Whether it is a romantic walk, or a walk with the entire family, end the night with a peaceful stroll down the beach – it will cap off your night, and your Shore vacation just right.

SOURCES

1. Wikipedia, Skee Ball. http://en.wikipedia.org/wiki/Skee_ball

2. National Horseshoes Pitchers Association. http://www.horseshoepitching.com/rules/PlayingRules.html

3. Wikipedia, Washers Pitching. http://en.wikipedia.org/wiki/Washer_pitching

4. Wikipedia, Cornhole. http://en.wikipedia.org/wiki/Cornhole

5. The Rules of Ladder Ball http://www.ladderball-rules.com/

6. eHow, How to Play Bocce Ball. http://www.ehow.com/how_3109_play-bocce-ball.html

7. Wikipedia, Disc Golf. http://en.wikipedia.org/wiki/Disc_golf

8. Song Lyrics, The Beach Boys – Catch a Wave Lyrics. http://www.songlyrics.com/beach-boys/catch-a-wave-lyrics/